LIVING
IN THE
SPIRIT

WITNESS LEE

Living Stream Ministry
Anaheim, CA • www.lsm.org

First Edition, March 2002.

ISBN 978-0-7363-0963-9

Published by

Living Stream Ministry
2431 W. La Palma Ave., Anaheim, CA 92801 U.S.A.
P. O. Box 2121, Anaheim, CA 92814 U.S.A.

Printed in the United States of America

15 16 17 18 19 20 / 10 9 8 7 6 5 4 3

CONTENTS

PREFACE

This book is composed of messages given in Chinese by Brother Witness Lee in an intensified training in life held in Taipei on August 19-23, 1975.

Ge 1.26-27 - and God said, Let
us make man in our image, after
our likeness; and let them have dominion
So God created man in his own image,
in the image of God created he him; male
female created he them.

Rev 4.3a - And He who sat there appeared
like a jasper + a sardine stone: ....

Rev 21.11,18 clothed in God's glory; and her
light was like unto a stone most precious,
even like a jasper stone, clear as crystal

and the bldg of the wall y it was of
jasper; and the city was pure gold
like unto clear glass.

*Ps 33.9 - He spoke - it was. He command
and it stood.

1.9 – ...I serve God with my spirit

m4.22 – The Lord JC be w your spirit

8.16 – The Spirit itself testifies 2gether c our spirit that we are children of God

rm 3.6 – ...that which is born of the Spirit is spirit

20.27 – The spirit of man is the candle of the Lord...

b 32.8 – But there is a spirit in man...

ch 12.1 – ...Thus says the Lord, who stretches out the heavens + lays the foundation of the earth + forms the Spirit of man within him.

e 2.7 – Then the Lord God formed man from the dust of the ground, and breathed into his nostrils the breath of life, + man became a living soul.

CHAPTER ONE

EXPRESSING GOD AND LIVING IN THE SPIRIT

Scripture Reading: Gen. 1:26-27; Eph. 4:24; Rev. 4:3a; 21:11,
18a; Gen. 2:7; Zech. 12:1b; Job 32:8a; Prov. 20:27a; John 3:6b;
Rom. 8:16; 2 Tim. 4:22; Rom. 1:9

r 4.24 ...put on the new man, which after God is called in h'teousness + true holiness.

THE CONSISTENT THOUGHT
IN THE SCRIPTURES

We all realize that the Bible is consistent, but what makes
it consistent? How does the Bible begin, develop, and end?
Some may say that Christ makes the Bible consistent. This
kind of reasoning, though, is too superficial. In this chapter
we will open up the "gold mine" of the Bible and excavate the
gold that is buried deep inside it. The Bible, like every object,
has two sides—the inside and the outside. For example, the
surface of this podium is dark brown. However, on the inside
its color is the color of wood. In order to see the color inside, we
must get below the surface.

At the (Beginning) of the Scriptures

The first mention of man in the Bible links man with the
image of God. In Genesis 1:26 God said, "Let Us make man in
Our image, according to Our likeness." Genesis 1 tells us that
in His creation God created numerous things over a period of
five days. During those five days He created everything by
speaking. God said, "Let there be light," and there was light
(v. 3). He said, "Let there be an expanse," and there was an
expanse (vv. 6-7). Psalm 33:9 says, "He spoke, and it was; / He
commanded, and it stood." However, on the sixth day God held
a conference of the Godhead. He said, "Let Us make man in

The counsel of the Lord

Our image, according to Our likeness." Prior to creating man, He created the heavens, the earth, and a myriad of items. However, these items were not His central purpose. His central purpose is fixed on man. God wants man to be His expression, so He created man according to His image. Hence, man is like a photograph of God. This photograph is God's picture, God's reprint, and God's expression.

Some of us may have heard or read numerous messages on this matter. However, regardless of how many times we have heard it, we still may not understand it because this matter does not exist in our natural concept. In the Scriptures there is the principle of first mention. According to this principle, the first mention of a matter in the Scriptures sets the principles of that particular matter for the entire Bible. The first mention of man in the Bible says that man was created according to the image of God; that is, man is God's expression, God's reprint, and God's manifestation. This is the principle. If you were to ask me why man was created, I would answer, "Man was created for God's expression." This is why man is like a photograph of God and a reprint of God. Obviously, those who do not believe in God and the Scriptures could not utter such a statement, and I believe that even many of those who have been in Christianity for years may not be able to utter it. We must see that the Bible reveals that God wants man to be His reprint. If nine hundred of us were to gather together, we would all look similar to each other. This is because we are all reprints of one original copy. Every one of us looks like God. Not one among us looks like a cow. Every one of us is a reprint of God to express God. This is what the Bible tells us at the beginning.

The Bible shows us that in the beginning God created the heavens and the earth and that on the first day He created one thing, on the second day He created another, and so on. After the heavens, the earth, the sun, the moon, the grass, the trees, and various creatures had been created, God said, "Let Us make man in Our image." This is God's central purpose, and this is the central thought that can be seen consistently throughout the Scriptures. God's intention is for man to be like Him and to express Him.

At the End of the Scriptures

At the end of the Scriptures in Revelation 21 and 22, a city appears. This city is not a physical city that is built up with material stones. It is a spiritual symbol describing an entity composed of redeemed, regenerated, and transformed people. It is a city of living people. This city is a living city built with living people as living stones. Each stone has the name of a person written on it, one stone bearing the name of Peter, another stone bearing the name of John, and so on. Hallelujah! We are all stones.

What is the purpose of this city? The wall of the city is a hundred and forty-four cubits in height, and every stone in the wall is jasper (21:17-18a). Furthermore, the city is full of God's glory (v. 11). What do these jasper stones signify? Revelation 4 reveals that God, who sits on the throne, is like a jasper stone in appearance (v. 3). John saw God sitting on the throne with the likeness of a jasper stone. Therefore, the fact that the wall of the city shines brightly like a jasper stone signifies that the city is the expression of God. God is first manifested on the throne and will eventually be manifested in the entire city.

This is the principle seen consistently throughout the Scriptures. The beginning of the Bible says that God created man so that man may be like Him. The end of the Bible says that God's redeemed, regenerated, and transformed people have corporately become like Him.

In the Middle of the Scriptures

What is in the middle of the Scriptures? In the Bible there is something called the old man and also something called the new man. Genesis 1 concerns the old man created by God, and Ephesians 4 concerns the new man. Ephesians 4 shows us that the new man, which is the church, was created according to God (v. 24). The old man was created according to the image of God, so the new man was also created according to the image of God (Col. 3:10). The ultimate manifestation of the new man in Ephesians 4 is the city, New Jerusalem, at the end of Revelation. The New Jerusalem is the aggregate of the new man and the ultimate manifestation of the new man. Therefore, in the beginning of the Bible man is the expression of God, in the middle of the Bible man is the expression of God, and also at the end of the Bible man is the expression of God. The Scriptures consistently show us that God desires to be expressed and that He does not want to be expressed merely through Himself. He wants to be expressed through man.

THE CORPORATE NEW MAN
AS THE EXPRESSION OF GOD

This expression is not individual but corporate. In the beginning when God created Adam, He did not create only one person. Rather, He created mankind. Adam was not an individual man but a corporate man, that is, mankind. Millions of Adam's descendants were included in him. Thus, God did not merely create an individual man; He created a corporate man. God does not want to be expressed merely through an individual. His desire is to have a corporate expression.

We often speak about the ground of the church. In order to see the matter of the ground of the church, we do not have to wait until Revelation 1. The ground of the church is already implied in Genesis 1:26. How can we say this? We can say this because in the beginning when God created man, He did not create two individuals. If He had created two individuals, there would have been two grounds on which to stand. In the beginning God created only one man. Genesis 5:2 says, "Male and female He created them...and called their name Adam, on the day when they were created." The male was named Adam, and the female was also named Adam. God did not create two persons. He created only one man. You may argue, saying that God created a male and a female. This is correct, yet the male and the female were just one person. From God's viewpoint, He created only one man.

We may have been born in the twentieth century, but when were we created? Were we created or born? We were all first created and then born, because when Adam was created, we also were created. Adam, Abel, Paul, and we were all created at the same time. The only difference is that Abel and

Paul were born earlier than we were. We were created at the same time but born at different times. This shows us that we are all on the same ground.

In Genesis 9, due to Satan's infiltration and man's fall, nations were formed. These nations typify today's denominations. However, in Acts on the day of Pentecost, people who had come to Jerusalem from different nations and who spoke different dialects were gathered together. There in Jerusalem, many of them received grace and the divine life and therefore were built together to become one new man. This new man is the church, which is for the expression of God.

GOD'S UNIQUE INTENTION
BEING FOR MAN TO EXPRESS HIM

The Scriptures consistently show us that the main thought in the Bible is that God wants man to express Him. Perhaps you may say that the Bible shows us that God wants us to worship Him, to serve Him, and to work for Him. The Bible certainly mentions these things, but you cannot find them in the first two chapters of Genesis. There is no thought of worshipping God, serving God, or working for God in these chapters. The only thought seen in them is that man was created in the image of God for His expression. Suppose I am a photograph of you, and as your photograph I begin to worship you, serve you, and work for you. You would think, "What a foolish picture! Everything it is doing is nonsense. I do not want my picture to worship me, serve me, or work for me. I just want my picture to express me in a clear way."

We must see that the consistent purpose, the central purpose, of God is not for us to worship Him, serve Him, or work for Him but for us to express Him. What God requires of the church in Taipei is not our zeal, devout worship, or successful service. Rather, God desires that people would see God when they come to Taipei. Every church needs to realize this. This is not a matter of our zeal, diligence, or devout worship but of our expressing God. When people come to our meetings, they should be able to declare that God is truly among us.

Degraded Christianity has deviated from the lofty goal and eternal purpose of God to being concerned merely with worshipping God, serving God, and working for God. Perhaps some would argue, saying, "Did Paul not tell us to worship God? Did he not tell us to serve God?" He certainly did, but we must realize that the worshipping, serving, and working for God spoken of by Paul are for the expression of Christ. We may be using the same terms as Paul, but our understanding of those terms may be different. The worshipping, serving, and working for God spoken of by Paul may not be what we think they are. If we would read through Paul's Epistles, we would see that what Paul meant by worshipping God, serving God, and working for God was to live out Christ and to live Christ in the presence of men.

The church is the new man, which is a photograph of God. God intends to have a photograph, a reprint, of Himself in this universe. When God Himself is reprinted, that reprint is the church. There are many different aspects of the church, and one of them is the church as the reprint of God. The church is a corporate picture of God. It is like a picture of God taken by God Himself. God has no intention for this picture to worship Him, serve Him, and work for Him. His only intention is that this picture would manifest Him in a clear and definite way so that when people see the church they would see Him. If people were to ask you, "Where is God?" you could say, "Come and see—God is in the church." If they were to ask, "What does God look like?" you could say, "When you see the church, you see God." In the early days those in the church in Jerusalem may have said, "O Jews! Do you want to know God? Then come and see the church. What your fathers passed on to you and what you learned from them was only the law in doctrine. Today, however, what is being expressed in the church in Jerusalem is the Lord Himself. The church in Jerusalem is a reprint of God." Can we say the same today? If we cannot say this, we are off.

The Scriptures show us that when God rebuked and judged His people, He often rebuked them not so much for their sins and evil doings but for being zealous in serving Him without expressing Him. Consider the seven epistles in Revelation. In the first epistle written to the messenger of the church in Ephesus, the Lord said, "I know your works and your labor and your endurance...and you...have borne all things because of My name and have not grown weary. But I have one thing against you, that you have left your first love...I am coming to you and will remove your lampstand out of its place, unless you repent" (2:2-5). What did the Lord mean? The Lord seemed to be saying, "You do not express Me. You care for works, for endurance, and for many other good things but not for Me. Since you do not care for Me, I do not care for you either."

Submit to Him

Our situation is often the same. For fifty years I could not change my concept. I constantly had the desire to work for God. I thought I was called by God, so I served God, worked for God, and worshipped God. We all have the same concept. Perhaps we may say to ourselves, "My prayers have not been devout enough, so today I will try to be more devout." However, God does not care for our devoutness, no matter how devout we are or how devout our prayers are. What then does God want? God wants us to express Him. If we have a sorrowful countenance, we have the expression of a beggar, not the expression of God. Perhaps we may think to ourselves, "Everyone around me is so careless. I am the only one who is careful. I never dare to say anything or make any move, lest I sin against God." Others' carelessness may not be worth anything, but in God's eyes, neither is our carefulness worth anything. People cannot see God in their carelessness; neither can they see God in your carefulness. God is not expressed through either of you because both of you are covered by a veil. The veil covering them is like a thin bridal veil, but the veil covering you is like a thick cow skin. Your piety is worthless, because when people see you, all they see is a sorrowful countenance. This is not what God wants. What God wants is to be expressed through us. Your sorrowful countenance will not lead people to salvation. Only the light of the expression of God through us will cause people to touch God.

EXPRESSING GOD BY USING OUR SPIRIT

In order to express God we must exercise our spirit. As humans, we have a spirit. In the beginning God created man in a particular way. God first used the dust of the ground to make a body as a frame, and then He breathed His breath into man (Gen. 2:7). The Hebrew word for *breath* here is also translated as "spirit" in Proverbs 20:27. There it says, "The spirit of man is the lamp of Jehovah." The same Hebrew word is translated as "spirit" in one place and as "breath" in another place. This proves that the breath that God breathed into man is related to the spirit of man. Man has been constructed in a special way. He has a spirit within him.

To illustrate this matter, let us consider a radio. A radio consists of a box on the outside and a device on the inside that is able to receive radio waves. If the device were removed, there would be no way for the radio to receive the radio waves that are in the air. The inward device is a special kind of construction. Similarly, each one of us has an invisible, intangible spirit within our visible, tangible body. We may already know this, but we may not know it in a thorough way. For many years I did not see that the spirit of man is as important as the heavens and the earth. Zechariah 12:1 says that Jehovah stretched forth the heavens, laid the foundations of the earth, and also formed a spirit within man. The heavens, the earth, and man are mentioned together. The heavens are for the earth, the earth is for man, and man is for God. Since God is Spirit, man must have a spirit within him. As Spirit, God is like the radio waves in the air—hard to describe or ascertain, yet very real. Man is for God. Therefore, man must have a spirit in order to contact God as Spirit. This is why Zechariah says that God created the heavens, the earth, and a spirit within man. What was the purpose of this? The purpose was for God to obtain a vessel in this universe that could contain Him and be His expression. The spirit of man is not only an organ to contact God but also a vessel to contain God. We may use the stomach as an illustration. The stomach is a vessel to contain food. Furthermore, it can digest the food that we eat and absorb and transport its nutrients to every part of our body. Just as we have a physical stomach, we also have a spiritual stomach in us—our spirit. Not only can our spirit contact God, but it can also store and contain God within. Furthermore, this spirit can assimilate and convey God to every part of our being.

NOT BEING RELIGIOUS BUT LIVING IN THE SPIRIT

Regrettably, many Christians simply do not understand the matter of the spirit. Most of the time we do not live in the spirit in our family life. Even in our meeting life, we still may not know how to use the spirit. In our meetings we may know how to use different methods, but we may not know how to use the spirit. Many of us may think that shouting in the meetings is the release of the spirit, yet we may not realize that shouting can become an ordinance, a method. If we shout and cry loudly but do not know our spirit, then whatever we do is still a method. Formerly we may have had meetings in an old way. This way was not of the spirit. Now we may have a new way. This way, however, is also not of the spirit. Actually, it is not difficult to have a proper meeting. The difficulty is that we do not have the right understanding, and we do not practice using our spirit. When we come to a meeting, we may have a set of routines—praying, singing, reading the Scriptures, giving a message, testifying, sharing, and fellowshipping. However, we may not prepare our spirit before coming to the meeting. We may even act like we do not have a spirit. We know how to use our eyes to look at things around us and also how to use our mind to think about certain matters; however, we may not know how to exercise our spirit. Formerly we may have been silent in the meetings, and currently we may shout in the meetings. However, if we do not exercise our spirit, there is no difference between the two. If you shout without using your spirit, then I cannot say Amen to your shouting, and if you do not exercise your spirit while you remain silent, I cannot say Amen to your silence. The problem is that in our meetings we often shout and cry without using our spirit. Outwardly we may shout and cry, yet inwardly our spirit may not be touched. Therefore, God is not expressed in our meetings.

Our normal practice should be to prepare and exercise our spirit before we come to the meeting. Once we exercise our spirit, we will forget about our thoughts. Once we exercise our spirit, we will forget about our feelings. In fact, once we exercise our spirit, we will forget about everything, even about asceticism → Severe self-discipline + avoidance of all forms of indulgence for religious reasons.

who we are. If we forget about everything to this extent, we will be almost completely in the spirit. Our spirit will be stirred up, and once we come to the meeting and sit down, the spirit of all those who are present will also be stirred up without our having to shout or cry.

We need to pray for the Lord's mercy. Almost everything that we are practicing today has become a religious practice. Christianity has turned the truths that are in the Scriptures into something of religion. For example, the Bible tells us to bear the cross. The bearing of the cross as seen in the Bible, however, can be carried out only in the spirit. When we are truly living in the spirit, we are bearing the cross. If we try to bear the cross without living in the spirit, we will be practicing a form of asceticism, which in principle is almost the same as Hinduism. A husband might say, "I know my wife is a cross given to me by the Lord, so I have to bear this cross." A wife might say, "My husband was given to me by the Lord, and I cannot ask for a divorce. This must be a cross from the Lord, so I will bear it. The Lord also gave me several children, so I have a big cross plus several little crosses." This is not what the Bible says regarding bearing the cross. Rather, the Bible says that we need to live in the spirit. If we have children, we need to live in the spirit, and if we do not have children, we also need to live in the spirit. If our children are obedient, we need to live in the spirit, and if they are disobedient, we still need to live in the spirit. As long as we live in the spirit, we will spontaneously bear the cross. To bear the cross is to deny our self and to give up our own choice. How can we deny our self? How can we allow the Lord to make choices for us? The only way is to live in the spirit.

If we would read the New Testament again, we would realize that in essence the New Testament teaches us simply to live in the spirit and to walk according to the spirit. The Bible never requires us to bear the cross while gnashing our teeth. We may even misunderstand the matter spoken of in Romans 6:11 concerning reckoning ourselves dead to sin. According to this verse, it is proper for us to reckon ourselves dead to sin. However, in our experience the more we reckon ourselves dead, the harder it is for us to die. This is because we may be trying to experience Romans 6 without having Romans 8. Romans 8 tells us to walk according to the spirit, to live in the spirit (v. 4). If we do not live in the spirit, although we may practice to pray more, we will still be practicing a kind of self-mortification or asceticism, which we can do for only so long. The Christian living is a living in the spirit. Only when we live in the spirit can we pray without ceasing. The secret of the Christian life is to live in the spirit.

THE REALITY OF THE CHURCH BEING PRESENT WHEN WE LIVE IN THE SPIRIT

To live in the spirit is not to engage in religious worship, religious service, or religious work. To live in the spirit is to let Christ fill and saturate us until He permeates our whole being and is thereby expressed through us. It is not a matter of husbands being able to love their wives or of wives being able to love their husbands. Rather, it is a matter of living in the spirit and allowing Christ as the life-giving Spirit to permeate our entire being and to express God through us. This is the overcoming life of a Christian, the family life of a Christian, and the church life of a Christian. This is the reality of the church. The reality of the church is to live in the spirit. The spirit that we are referring to is not merely the Holy Spirit but is our created and regenerated spirit. Today we need to forget about our thoughts, feelings, and everything else. We need to turn to our spirit and pay attention to being in our spirit. Most people pay attention to their mind and their feelings, but very few people pay attention to being in the spirit. We all need to be absorbed with being in spirit. We may not know what it is to bear the cross, but we should know what it is to follow the spirit. We may not know what it means to pray and to fast, or we may not know what it means to be humble and to be patient. However, we should know how to follow the spirit. When we follow the spirit, we have humility and patience, and we spontaneously bear the cross. Once we follow the spirit, all things are ours.

May the Lord open our eyes so that we may see the consistent truth in the Bible and see that the way to live in this truth is to live in the spirit. It was in our spirit that we were regenerated, and it is in our spirit that the Spirit of God is with us. It is in our spirit that the all-inclusive Christ dwells, and it is in our spirit that we enjoy His grace. It is in our spirit that we have His presence, and it is in our spirit that we have light, life, and truth. Everything is in our spirit.

CHAPTER TWO

THE LORD BEING THE SPIRIT IN OUR SPIRIT

Scripture Reading: Isa. 9:6; 2 Cor. 3:17; 1 Cor. 15:45b; Rom. 8:15; Gal. 4:6; Rom. 8:10; 2 Tim. 4:22; Rom. 8:4; Gal. 5:16, 25

THE TRIUNE GOD—
THE FATHER, THE SON, AND THE SPIRIT

Many of the saints in the Lord's recovery today still have not dropped their human concepts, cultural influences, and religious thoughts, not to mention the traditional teachings of Christianity. This is why there has not been much result even though we have released many things that God has shown us. The saints have heard what we have released, and they have seemed to receive it, yet there has not been much response in the church life in reality.

Suppose we told people that we were once fallen, but that God, who loved the world, came to be our Savior, and as our Savior died on the cross and shed His precious blood for the redemption of our sins. If we spoke in this way to people, it would be easy for them to comprehend because this kind of speaking not only corresponds to the Scriptures but also matches their natural concept. This kind of thought is very similar to the concept in the human mind. Hence, when we speak in this way, it is easy for people to understand, receive, and respond to our speaking. Suppose we also told them, "Since you have been saved, you need to have a change in your behavior. Before you were saved, your conduct was very poor, and it did not glorify God. Today, however, you have been saved and have become children of God, and now you need to behave yourself in a proper way. If you cannot do it, you need to pray. Then God will lend you a hand and will enable you to be a good person." This kind of teaching also conforms to man's frame of mind, so man easily receives it and is stirred up by it. This kind of teaching is also found in the Bible.

However, everything has two sides—a surface and an inside—and what is on the surface is often different from what is on the inside. The concepts described in the previous paragraph can be said to be on the surface of what is revealed in the Bible. They are not on the "inside." Then what is on the inside? Intrinsically, the Bible shows us that God is Spirit. God is not only Spirit in His essence, but He is also the Father, the Son, and the Spirit in His economy. God's being the Father, the Son, and the Spirit is not merely so that we can have the doctrine of the Trinity but is for God's economy. What is God's economy? God's economy is to work Himself into man. In order to dispense Himself into man, God has to be the Father, the Son, and the Spirit.

THE SON BEING THE FATHER AND ALSO THE SPIRIT

Traditional Christianity teaches the doctrine concerning the Trinity, saying that God is one yet has three persons. This teaching is not wrong, but it can be understood in a wrong way. In degraded Christianity many people who teach this doctrine have the hidden concept that the Father, the Son, and the Spirit are three Gods. It is a very serious mistake to have this kind of concept. Apparently these ones believe that God is uniquely one, but if we converse with them at length, eventually they will disclose what they truly believe. They believe that the Father is a God, the Son is a God, and the Spirit is a God. They believe that there are three Gods. Of course, most will not say this explicitly, but when we speak with some believers, we realize that inwardly they do not believe that the Son is the Father or that the Son is the Spirit. If we were to ask them how many Gods they believe in, they would eventually have to confess that they believe in three Gods.

This matter has been an issue of great controversy in theology throughout the years. However, we must realize that God in His trinity—the Father, the Son, and the Spirit—is not for doctrinal study but for the dispensing of God into us.

We should be very careful not to think that there are three Gods—the Father being one God, the Son being another God, and the Spirit being still another God. This is altogether a traditional concept that must be cast into the Pacific Ocean. This traditional concept is prevalent not only in China but also in America. In fact, most of the traditional Christian concepts came to China from the Western world. Today we are still fighting this battle in America. I have been challenging Christianity both privately and publicly concerning the traditional Christian concepts. For instance, I have challenged many of the Christians in America to explain how they understand Isaiah 9:6. That verse says, "A child is born to us, / A Son is given to us;... / And His name will be called / Wonderful Counselor, / Mighty God, / Eternal Father, / Prince of Peace." Most Christians do not have a problem with the names Wonderful Counselor, Prince of Peace, or Mighty God. They only have a problem with the name Eternal Father. Isaiah 9:6 speaks about One who is so wonderful that His name is called Wonderful. Furthermore, He is so wonderful that even though He is a child, His name is called Mighty God. Fundamental Christians today all believe that the child who was born in the manger in Bethlehem was the mighty God. That child was called Jesus, and He was God. If someone does not believe in this, we cannot acknowledge him as our brother. Instead, we would have to consider him an antichrist. Judaism believes in God but does not believe that that child was the mighty God. We, however, believe this.

In Isaiah 9:6 there are two lines—one line is the line of the child, and the other is the line of the Son. A child was born to us, and His name was called Mighty God, and a Son was given to us, and His name was called Eternal Father. Today, however, those in Christianity believe the first line but not the second line. If we were to ask them whether the child born in the manger was the mighty God, they would strongly answer that He was. If, however, we asked them whether the Son given to us was the eternal Father, they would not dare to answer. Even many pastors would not dare to answer, because many of them are under the influence of traditional teachings. Therefore, when I visited America, I strongly asked, "Should we believe only half of Isaiah 9:6, or should we believe the whole verse?" If we believe that the child is the mighty God, we should also believe that the Son is the eternal Father.

If anyone condemns us of being heretical because we say that the Son is the Father, we should show them Isaiah 9:6 and read it to them. When I was in the United States, I taught the brothers and sisters there a very simple strategy of how to deal with these ones. First, we should ask them whether they believe that the Bible is true. If they do, we should ask them whether they believe that the book of Isaiah is true. If they do, then we should ask them whether they believe that Isaiah 9:6 is true. If they say that they do, then we should ask them whether they believe that the child is the mighty God. If they still say yes, we should ask them whether they also believe that the Son is the eternal Father. In this way we will stop all their arguments. We should not argue with such people, because the more we argue, the more they will become confused, and the more they will argue with us. We do not need to say anything except to ask them these few questions. Then they will be unable to do anything except acknowledge that the Son is the eternal Father. There are many deep things pertaining to God that are beyond our understanding. However, every Christian must accept the plain words of the Bible. This is the first step.

The second step is to show them 2 Corinthians 3:17, which says, "The Lord is the Spirit." We should ask them whether the Lord in this verse refers to the Lord Jesus. They will surely say yes. No one would say that the Lord in this verse is not the Lord Jesus. The Lord mentioned here is the Lord Jesus (cf. 4:5). Then we should ask them who the Spirit in this verse refers to. They would have to admit that the Spirit mentioned here is the Holy Spirit. There would then be no need for further argument. We could also show them 1 Corinthians 15:45b, which says, "The last Adam became a life-giving Spirit." This is also irrefutable.

The critics will surely ask many other questions. They may ask, "If you say that the Son is the Father, then how could the Son pray to the Father? And how could the Father hear the Son's prayer?" We can tell them that we do not know how to answer, and neither do we want to. However, we can ask them to explain John 14, where the Lord said to Philip, "Have I been so long a time with you, and you have not known Me, Philip? He who has seen Me has seen the Father;...I am in the Father and the Father is in Me" (vv. 9-10). We should not try to explain, because eventually we will become confused and will be unable to fight the battle. However, Isaiah 9:6 is very clear, as is 2 Corinthians 3:17. One verse says that the Son would be called the Father, and the other verse says that the Lord is the Spirit.

In one of his hymns, Brother Nee said, "Thou, Lord, the Father once wast called, / But now the Holy Spirit art" (*Hymns,* #490, stanza 5). This shows that Brother Nee saw this matter a long time ago.

I am not here to argue about doctrines but to give you an impression. We all need to see that our God is one and that this one God, as the mysterious One, is the Father, the Son, and the Spirit. He is the Father for a reason, He is the Son with an intention, and He is the Spirit for a purpose. The reason, intention, and purpose are that He would fully work Himself into us.

THE TRIUNE GOD AS THE SPIRIT
DWELLING IN OUR SPIRIT

We must look to the Lord that He would enable us to see clearly that today our God, our Redeemer, is the Spirit. In His essence He is Spirit, in His economy He is ultimately the Spirit, and in His resurrection He actually became the Spirit. Not only did He become flesh to accomplish redemption for us; He also became the Spirit to come into us to be our life. We must see that today our God, our Redeemer, is the wonderful, all-inclusive Spirit. This wonderful Spirit is not only in the third heaven but is also dwelling specifically in our spirit.

Romans 8 says that Christ is in us, and that as a result, our spirit is life (v. 10). Today Christ as the Spirit is in our spirit, so our spirit, which contains Him as life, is life. We may use electricity to illustrate this. When electricity enters into a light bulb, the light bulb becomes light. This revelation of our spirit being life is made crystal clear in the New Testament. The Lord who became flesh, who died and shed His blood for the forgiveness of sins, and who was resurrected is now the Spirit. He is not only with us in our spirit but is also mingled with our spirit as one spirit. This truth has been taught among us for many years, and this message has been released numerous times. However, there has not been much response or practical application because we are still very much limited by old concepts, old backgrounds, and other teachings.

Recently, I attended a Lord's Day meeting in which a message was given on the topic of "pressing on" based on Philippians 3:13-14 (ASV). The message was about pressing on, the saints sang hymns about pressing on, and many of the saints were shouting, "Press on!" However, much of the shouting was natural and without revelation, and thus, the brothers and sisters who attended that meeting left without receiving any help. In that meeting there was much talk about pressing on, yet no one explained how to press on, where to start pressing on, and where to press on to. There was much shouting of words but no revelation. As I was listening there, I wondered, "Where are the ones sharing these things going to lead the church? Are they going to lead the church into the matter of pressing on?" It is true that Philippians 3:13-14 contains the thought of pressing on. However, we need to read through Philippians 3 before we can understand what it means to press on. To press on is to put away religion. Paul said, "Beware of the dogs...beware of the concision. For we are the circumcision, the ones who serve by the Spirit of God...and have no confidence in the flesh...If any other man thinks that he has confidence in the flesh, I more: circumcised the eighth day;...a Hebrew born of Hebrews; as to the law, a Pharisee; as to zeal, persecuting the church; as to the righteousness which is in the law, become blameless. But what things were gains to me, these I have counted as loss on account of Christ...I have suffered the loss of all things and count them as refuse that I may gain Christ" (vv. 2-8). Instead of merely shouting about forgetting the things behind, we need to realize what the things behind are and what the things we need to forget are. If we had the revelation, we would realize that the things which are behind are things such as our religious concepts, our keeping of the law, and our zeal. We need to forget about our service as a responsible one in a small group, in a home meeting, or in a meeting hall. We need to forget about being so busy and working so hard to carry out those responsibilities. From where do we start to press on? We need to start by forgetting about our responsibilities in the home meetings and our busyness. We should not turn Philippians 3:13-14 into mere slogans, shouting things such as, "Forgetting the things which are behind," "Stretching forward to the things which are before," and, "Press on toward the goal." What is our goal? Our goal is Christ, who is in our spirit. In that Lord's table meeting, why is it that no one declared, "Press on to the spirit! Our goal is the spirit!" The goal is not in our responsibility or in our service. The goal is Christ, who is in our spirit. We may have heard this message many times, yet in our practical application we have failed. We have heard the truth, but we have not seen the revelation.

If we have truly seen the revelation, we should be able to give ten thousand messages, each with a different subject yet with the same principle. However, if we speak about pressing on without having seen the revelation, then the church will not be edified, because our leading of the church will have no direction or goal. What should our direction be? Our direction and our goal should be the Christ who lives in our spirit. We can speak this message and apply it to thousands of matters, even to the way we cut our hair. Whether we should leave our hair long or cut our hair short is not a matter of regulation. We should not inquire of the elders or search the Scriptures concerning such a matter. Instead, we should inquire of our spirit and turn to our spirit. We should not promote short hair or long hair. Instead, we should turn to our spirit! Whatever message we speak, this should be the principle.

Those without this vision are groping in the dark and speaking nonsense. We may speak about prayer—how to pray and what to pray—but unless we have seen this vision, our prayers will be nonsensical prayers. Before he was saved, Saul of Tarsus probably prayed more than any of us. After receiving the letters from the high priest and while he was on his way to Damascus to arrest the saints, he must have intensified his prayers and prayed thoroughly. Yet his prayers were in cooperation with Satan. He was praying to God, yet he was being utilized by Satan. Whoever has not seen this vision is liable to fall into the scheme of Satan, no matter what he does.

THE WONDERFUL SPIRIT AS THE KEY TO EVERYTHING

We need to see this vision. We need to see that the Triune God, the almighty God, who is Jehovah—the Father, the Son, and the Spirit, has become our all and has been wrought into us. Today He is in our spirit. The key to everything is found in this wonderful Spirit who is in our created and regenerated spirit and who has become one spirit with our spirit. This is the key and the starting point. If we do not turn to our spirit and pray out of our spirit, our prayers will be improper. If we do not enter into the mingled spirit and love others out of the mingled spirit, our love will be worthless. Anything that is not of the spirit is of the flesh and will not yield the fruit of the Holy Spirit. The Spirit of life will not confirm anything that is of the flesh.

We should forget about old religion. Having morning watch is worthless and praying is useless if we are not in the spirit. It is possible that our prayers have been in cooperation with Satan, that our morning watch has been infiltrated by Satan, and that even our service as an elder has been for Satan. This is not to say that we have brought idols into the church or have brought the brothers into sin. On the contrary, we may be very pious and diligent in leading the saints to have morning watch, to endeavor in this practice, and to endeavor in reading the Word. However, we may not realize that Satan has infiltrated all these things. There is only one place that Satan cannot invade—our spirit.

May the Lord be merciful to every one of us and grant us the heavenly vision. Do not think that merely being zealous and serving God is sufficient. Saul of Tarsus was also zealous and also served God, yet he was under the authority of Satan. His service to God, his zeal, and his keeping of the law were all under Satan's authority. Can we say that our zeal, our having morning watch, and our endeavoring in doing many things are not under Satan's authority? Whether or not we are under Satan's authority is not determined by the things we do. Rather, it is determined by whether we are in the spirit or in the flesh. Do we have morning watch in our natural being or in our spirit? If we have morning watch in our natural being, then even though we may rise at 5:30 A.M., our morning watch can be utilized by Satan. However, if we have morning watch in the spirit, there will be a different flavor.

We need to turn to our spirit. Being holy, victorious, or freed from sin is not what matters. The only thing that matters is that we live in the spirit where the Lord dwells.

CARING FOR NOTHING OTHER THAN LIVING IN THE SPIRIT

In the history of Christianity there have been many doctrinal teachings on matters such as bearing the cross, dealing with the flesh, pursuing holiness, living a victorious life, and being filled with the Holy Spirit. However, if we calmly and objectively read through the New Testament, then we would see that the crucial point of the New Testament is ultimately to be in the spirit. The book of Romans presents a general outline of the Christian life and the church life. Although chapter 6 mentions the cross, chapter 6 is not the end of the book. Chapter 8 repeatedly mentions the spirit. Chapter 6 directly refers to the cross only once (v. 6), but chapter 8 mentions the spirit over twenty times. Galatians also mentions the cross. However, Galatians also says, "Walk by the Spirit and you shall by no means fulfill the lust of the flesh" (5:16). If we attempt to deal with the flesh and crucify it while neglecting to be in the spirit, then the more we try to crucify the flesh, the more alive it will become. It is clear from Galatians that if we walk by the Spirit, we shall by no means fulfill the lust of the flesh. If we walk by the Spirit, we will be crucified without trying to be crucified, and we will be holy without trying to be holy. We will be victorious without trying to be victorious, we will love others without trying to love them, and we will have light without trying to obtain it. This is possible because the all-inclusive Spirit dwells in our spirit and has become one spirit with our spirit.

Today we all need to see this heavenly vision. If we see this, we will no longer care about being holy, being victorious, bearing the cross, and various other matters. We will care only to live in the spirit. In addition, if we live by the spirit, we should also walk by the spirit. As long as we walk in the spirit, nothing is impossible. However, if we do not walk in the spirit and try to crucify ourselves by exercising our will, then the more we try to crucify ourselves, the more alive we will be. If we practice dealing with the world by ourselves, then the more we try, the more we will love the world.

We should look to the Lord to have mercy on us and to open our eyes that we may see a heavenly vision. We need to see that the great God—Jehovah, the One who is the Father, the Son, and the Spirit, and who is also the Lord Jesus, the Redeemer, the Creator, and the Holy Spirit—is the all-inclusive Spirit who dwells in our spirit and is being mingled with our spirit as one spirit. This is where we should live and walk today. This should not be our performance but our daily living. We should live our daily life in the spirit. We should not be concerned with knowing what humility is or what love is. Neither should we be concerned with knowing what patience is, what submission is, what zeal is, what worship is, or what prayer is. We should not be concerned with anything other than living in the spirit. We should walk in the spirit day by day, simply being in harmony with our Lord and one with Him in the spirit. We should have our life, nature, living, and walk with our Lord. We do not need to know what prayer is or what to pray about. We do not need to know what gospel preaching is or what kind of gospel to preach. We do not need to know what it means to love our wife or to submit to our husband. Neither do we need to know what it means to be humble or patient. All these words and phrases are expressions used by moralists. The only thing we need to know is that the God and Savior whom we love is the all-inclusive life-giving Spirit who is dwelling in our spirit and has become one spirit with our spirit. We are joined to Him, and He is our life, our living, and our walk. He and we are one.

HAVING EVERYTHING BY LIVING IN THE SPIRIT

If the Lord is merciful to open your eyes and show you this matter, your entire Christian life will have a great turn. We should all read the Bible again. Ultimately, the entire Bible requires only one thing of us—to walk according to the mingled spirit, which is the all-inclusive Spirit mingled with our regenerated spirit. First Corinthians 6:17 tells us, "He who is joined to the Lord is one spirit." If our disposition is manifested, this proves that we are not in spirit. If we criticize and judge carelessly, this also proves that we are not in spirit. If we gossip freely, always hold on to our opinions, or insist on our views, then we are not in spirit. If we insist on having morning watch while others are not having morning watch, we are not in spirit. Then what does it mean to be in spirit? To be in spirit is simply to be in spirit, and to not be in spirit is simply to not be in spirit. We need to see that the reality of all spiritual things is in the spirit. The church itself is in the spirit, the building of the church is in the spirit, and the eternal testimony of the church is in the spirit. This is the hinge, the secret, and the key to our Christian life and our church life.

In the New Testament nearly no other item is mentioned more than the spirit. The New Testament speaks of the Spirit and the Spirit of life. It also mentions our regenerated spirit, and even more, it speaks of the spirit that is the mingling of the Spirit with our spirit. The New Testament repeatedly refers to this spirit. Nearly every book speaks about this spirit. Revelation, the last book of the Bible, especially shows us that we need to be in this spirit (1:10; 4:2; 17:3; 21:10). We must see that today in the church we also need to emphasize the spirit. The more we speak about other things, the more deadened and empty we will be, and the more others will not want to listen. The age we are in today is the age of the spirit, an age in which there is the flow of the spirit.

May the Lord be merciful to us that our eyes may be opened to see the spirit. I have seen many different things in Christianity. I was with the Brethren assembly for seven and a half years, I have been with the Pentecostal movement, and I have been in the line of the inner life. I know with assurance that there is no other way besides this. This is the Lord's way today. Only in the spirit can we enter into the riches of the Lord, and only in the spirit can we be delivered from everything outside of the Lord. May the Lord have mercy on us that we would all see this spirit.

CHAPTER THREE

GOD AND MAN LIVING TOGETHER
AND LIVING IN THE SPIRIT

Scripture Reading: John 1:14, 18; 6:57; 14:7-9, 16a, 17, 19-20, 23; 15:5; 17:21a, 23a; 20:22; 3:6b; 4:24

Let us now consider the Gospel of John. Although this book is familiar to us, most Christians, including many of us, do not realize what the spirit, the reality, or the essence of the Gospel of John is. Although we have released numerous messages based on this book and have spent a great deal of effort to study it, most of us who are in the churches have not realized the essence of the Gospel of John.

Most Christians' knowledge of the Gospel of John is limited to the following points: First, "Behold, the Lamb of God, who takes away the sin of the world!" (1:29); second, "God so loved the world" (3:16); and third, "I am the good Shepherd; the good Shepherd lays down His life for the sheep" (10:11). Some have also seen that we have received a new commandment to love one another (13:34). Others have seen that since we love one another, we should wash one another's feet (v. 14). Still others have seen even more, realizing that the Lord is the vine, that we are the branches, and that we abide in Him and He in us (15:1, 4-5). However, most of them do not understand how we can abide in Him and how He can abide in us. They have some amount of knowledge but very little experience. Still others have seen the Lord's prayer for oneness in John 17. As a whole, this is the extent of most Christians' knowledge of the Gospel of John. If this is our case, this indicates that we do not realize what the essence of the Gospel of John is.

The Gospel of John mainly speaks about God. John 1:1 says, "In the beginning was the Word, and the Word was with

God, and the Word was God." Hence, the Gospel of John is a book concerning God, not man. Its purpose in speaking about God is to show us that God has a heart's desire, which is to work Himself into man. Its intention is not to teach us how to worship and serve God, how to work for God, or how to improve ourselves so that we could become noble people. There is no such thing in the Gospel of John. Among the sixty-six books of the Bible, the Gospel of John speaks exclusively concerning one thing: God intends to work Himself into man to be man's life and life supply. Moreover, He wants to be altogether one with man. Because He desires to enter into us and to put us into Himself, we should abide in Him, and then He will also abide in us. Not only so, He and we, we and He, will live together. He will come into us to abide with us. He also wants us to live by Him and with Him.

The highest gospel is not merely concerning the forgiveness of sins and deliverance from hell so that we may receive eternal blessing. Rather, the highest gospel is that we would be saved to the extent that God and we, we and God, are completely mingled as one, having one life and one living. We were fallen sinners—wicked, degraded, evil, and desolate— yet we can have one life and one living with God. God can abide with us and live with us. Do we believe this? If we do believe this, it may be our belief in theory but not be our living. We may have been Christians for decades, yet we may have never had the deep realization that the gospel of God saves us into Him to live with Him so that He and we can have one life and one living. We may have read the Bible every day and read the Gospel of John several times, yet we may have never had this concept. What have we seen in the Gospel of John? We may have seen the sweetness of the Lord Jesus in His words, acts, and conduct. Nevertheless, regardless of how sweet He is, He is still He, and we are still we. We should read John 15:4, which says, "Abide in Me and I in you." We should read John 6:57, which says, "As the living Father has sent Me and I live because of the Father, so he who eats Me, he also shall live because of Me." These words are much deeper, showing us that the Lord is not only near us but is also mingled with us.

GOD ENTERING INTO MAN
TO HAVE ONE LIFE AND ONE LIVING WITH MAN

We should not treat this matter as a doctrine. Rather, we should all receive a real impression. We want to see a mysterious vision in the Gospel of John. What is a vision, and what is a revelation? If I were to cover my face with a veil, you would be unable to see my face. Thus, there would be no revelation. Revelation is like the removing of the veil to expose my face. However, if there was revelation but no light or sight, you still would be unable to see my face. You would know that something has been revealed, but you would not know what that thing was. If there was light here and you also had sight, then upon removing the veil, you would immediately see my face. My face would be a vision to you. A vision is a scene that is uncommon or extraordinary.

The Gospel of John is a book of revelation. However, we need the light to shine on the revelation, and we also need the sight to see. Therefore, we need to look to the Lord. The revelation of the Gospel of John has been opened. However, we still need the Lord's shining, and we also need the Lord to give us spiritual sight so that we may see the scene in this book and receive a vision.

The Gospel of John is about God, who is the Creator of all things. The purpose of this book is to show how this God works Himself into man. How does God accomplish this? The best way for us to take something into us is by eating it. Does God then need to divide Himself into tiny pieces? Initially, there was no way for us to eat God, because as the Creator, God is mysterious, incomprehensible, great, and glorious. If He came to us as the Creator, we would fall down in fear and trembling. Therefore, the Gospel of John reveals that first the Word was God: "In the beginning was the Word,...and the Word was God" (1:1). What are words for? Words are for expression and explanation. In the book of John, the mysterious and hidden God is expressed as the Word. As the Word, Christ speaks forth and expresses the mysterious and hidden God. If someone does not know God, he only needs to come to Christ, who is the explanation of God. Second, God became flesh, a man (v. 14). The great and glorious God became a man so that men could

draw near to Him without fear. Third, this God in the flesh
was the Lamb. Man is sinful, but God is holy, and God cannot
contact anything that has sin. Hence, as the Lamb of God He
carried our sins to the cross and dealt with them there. On
the cross He accomplished redemption by the shedding of His
blood, and then He was buried. Then, something wonderful
transpired, something that had never occurred in human history. After His burial He resurrected, and in His resurrection
He still had a human body, but He also became the Spirit.
Then He came to where the disciples were, and even though
the doors were shut, He entered without knocking on the door
and without anyone opening the door for Him. Actually, He
did not even enter the room; He simply came and stood in their
midst (20:19). His mysterious body is simply beyond our com-
prehension. As He was standing in the midst of the disciples,
He did not preach to them or give them a teaching. Instead, He
breathed into them and said to them, "Receive the Holy Spirit"
(v. 22). In this way He entered into them. God entered into the
disciples to become one with them. The two—God and man,
man and God—became one, having one life and one living.
Through the Spirit, God can live in man, and man can live by
God.

The Gospel of John clearly tells us that God is Spirit (4:24).
Because He is Spirit, He can enter into man. Long before He
entered into man, He prepared a spirit for man. Man has a
spirit within him. This book tells us that the spirit within
man needs regeneration (3:6). It needs to be regenerated with
God as the divine Spirit. In this way the divine Spirit can be
begotten in the spirit of man. Not only so, this book tells us
that this God as the mysterious One is not only our life but
also our bread of life (6:35). Hence, we can eat Him and take
Him into us. However, we do not eat Him in the same way that
we eat bread. The Lord said, "It is the Spirit who gives life;...
the words which I have spoken to you are spirit and are life"
(v. 63). This means that we need to receive the Lord's words
with our spirit. Then we will have Him, and He will be the life
within us. Eventually, He said that those who eat Him will
live because of Him (v. 57). We do not live by ourselves but by
the Spirit whom we have received.

We must see what kind of book the Gospel of John is. It shows us that after going through the process of incarnation, death, and resurrection, God became the all-inclusive life-giving Spirit. All we need to do is exercise our spirit to receive Him. Then He enters into our spirit to be mingled with us as one spirit. He becomes our life and life supply, and we live by Him. The two—He and we, we and He—have one life, one living, and one walk.

GOD AND MAN LIVING TOGETHER
BEING A MATTER OF THE SPIRIT

In John 15 the Lord said, "Abide in Me and I in you" (v. 4). How can we abide in Him, and how can He abide in us? This is altogether a matter of the spirit. Because He is the Spirit, we can abide in Him, and He can also abide in us. Today we all abide in the air, and the air also abides in us. In the Scriptures air is a type of the Spirit. Furthermore, in the Old Testament *air* and *spirit* are denoted by the same Hebrew word, and in the New Testament they are denoted by the same Greek word. The Lord Jesus breathed into His disciples and said to them, "Receive the Holy Spirit" (20:22). It would be quite appropriate to translate the Lord's word into, "Receive the Holy Breath." The Spirit is the breath. Our Lord today is the holy breath. This is why today we can abide in the Lord, and the Lord can also abide in us.

If we would read the Gospel of John as someone who has never heard the gospel or has never read the Bible before, we would see something wonderful. We would see that after doing so many things, God became a wonderful Spirit, and that He has breathed Himself into us. We would also see that we have a spirit to receive Him into us. In our spirit we have been regenerated. In our spirit we can contact Him. In our spirit we can live by Him. In our spirit we can abide in Him, and in our spirit He can abide in us.

NEEDING ONLY TO LIVE IN THE SPIRIT
AND BY THE LORD

Most of us are clear about this matter. Regrettably, however, when it comes to our practical living, most of the time we do not consider the Gospel of John. For example, suppose I wake up one morning and remember the word in Ephesians that says that husbands should love their wives. I begin to pray, "Lord, I agree that husbands should love their wives, but, Lord, You know that I am weak and that I cannot love. Please help me, and as the Holy Spirit move me!" Suppose I have a very good morning watch that morning, but as a result, I am delayed and arrive ten minutes late for breakfast. As soon as my wife sees me, she says, "What is the matter with you? Where did you go? Do you not know what time it is?" Then immediately I respond, saying, "This is a cross from the Lord. I must bear the cross!" Upon hearing this, my wife becomes so angry that she scolds me and even throws chopsticks at me. "What do you mean by bearing the cross?" she asks. Then I may say within myself, "Oh, I need to receive the discipline of the Holy Spirit. I need this knife. I have many sharp places in my being. My parents did not teach me properly, so now I need my wife to teach me. Oh, I should pick up the cross! I should receive the discipline of the Holy Spirit!" Then I simply skip breakfast and hurriedly go to work while in my heart all I can think about is bearing the cross and receiving the discipline of the Holy Spirit. However, at noontime, the more I think about the situation, the angrier I become, thinking, "She should not have thrown chopsticks at me!" Then I tell myself, "It is not right to think this way. I must pray! I must be watchful and pray that I may not fall into temptation." Therefore, I pray, "O Lord, keep me from falling into temptation!" When I return home after work, my wife is still angry with me. When she sees me, the first words she says are, "Have you had enough bearing of the cross yet? Have you learned the lesson of being disciplined by the Holy Spirit?" Sometimes the Lord allows Satan to bother us in this way.

There are different ways of looking at all our situations. We may think that all the things that happen to us are lessons from God. However, if we had the light from the Gospel of John, we would see things from another angle and realize that it is not a matter of "learning lessons." We would see that all the things that happen to us test us as to whether we are living in the spirit or in our self. When you are truly living in the spirit, there is no need to bear the cross, to be broken, or to be disciplined by the Holy Spirit. Even if your wife were to create a big uproar, you would not be bothered but would simply live in the spirit. If your wife gave you chicken soup, you would say, "Hallelujah." If she gave you plain water, you would also say, "Hallelujah." You would simply be living in the spirit. If you try to bear the cross and receive the discipline of the Holy Spirit without living in the spirit, you will only stir up your wife to give you more discipline. The devil knows how to deal with us. When we resist losing our temper, the devil will bother us again and again until we cannot help losing our temper. Under the devil's constant bothering, one day we will throw chopsticks at our wife. Then she will be happy and say, "So you also throw chopsticks! Now we are the same!" The best way to silence Satan is to live in the spirit. The best way is not pretending, being patient, "learning lessons," or being broken. We should not know anything except to live in the spirit. Today our Lord lives in our spirit, and we should live by Him. When we are rebuked, we should live by Him. When we are embraced and kissed, we should live by Him. When we are slapped on the face, we should still live by Him.

Do not think that these are just my words. The Lord said in the Gospel of John, "He who eats Me, he also shall live because of Me" (6:57). We should live by Him, not for only twenty minutes a day but for all twenty-four hours. It should not be that when our wife kisses us, we live by Him, but when she scolds us, we endure and bear the cross. It should not be that when we go into a department store, we quickly pray and become watchful in order that we would not fall into temptation. Rather, we should live by Him when we enter the meeting hall, and we should also live by Him when we enter the department store. Whether we have John 3 in front of us or a variety of things in front of us, we should live by Him. Outwardly our situations may change, but inwardly we should always be in a condition of living by Him.

LIVING IN THE SPIRIT BEING THE HIGHEST TEACHING

The highest teaching in the Scriptures is to live in the spirit. In the last few centuries this matter has never been released in such a clear way as it has been at this time. Pursuing holiness, pursuing victory, bearing the cross, and receiving the discipline of the Holy Spirit are all matters in the Scriptures. However, these matters are all branches. The trunk, the foundation, is living in the spirit. The reason we pursue holiness is because we do not live in the spirit. If we would live in the spirit, it would be unnecessary to pursue holiness. The reason we try to be patient and victorious is because we do not live in the spirit. If we would live in the spirit, pursuing patience and victory would be unnecessary. The reason we need to be dealt with by the cross is because we live in the self. However, if we would live in the spirit, there would be no need of dealing when we encounter the cross. The dealing of the cross is for us to live in the spirit. When we endeavor to be dealt with by the cross apart from the spirit, we are merely changing our understanding of a situation. For example, perhaps a brother has wronged us, lied about us, or offended us. At first we may be unable to get over it, but later we may think, "Now I realize that the Lord is dealing with me in this way to break me. I am a stubborn old man, and no one can do anything about me. Therefore, God has given me such a brother. Thank the Lord, my understanding has changed. I do not blame that brother anymore. Now I understand that God is using that brother as an ax to break me. Therefore, Father, I thank You. I would like to kiss the ax." We may have a change in understanding, but we still are not living in the spirit. We may endeavor to bear the cross three times in a day, but we still do not live in the spirit for even five minutes.

God does not want us to pursue holiness, victory, the cross, or breaking. God wants to be our life so that we may live by Him. I hope that a great light would shine here to tear down all those other teachings. We do not need to learn this lesson or that lesson. We need the spirit, and we need to live in the spirit. In a sense, God does not need a person who has been broken or who has been polished. God needs a person who lives by Him. God does not need a person who lives by Him for five minutes and then stops living by Him after five minutes. God needs people who will day and night, twenty-four hours a day, live in the spirit, live by Him, and live with Him as life.

Why then does the Bible contain so many other teachings? The other teachings are tests to determine whether or not we are living in the spirit. We should not be mistaken into thinking that those teachings in the Bible are meant for us to practice. They are there to prove whether or not we are living in the spirit. The Gospel of John does not teach us to be humble, to be patient, to bear the cross, or to learn this lesson or that lesson. The main emphasis of the Gospel of John can be found in three verses: "He who eats Me, he also shall live because of Me" (6:57); "Abide in Me and I in you" (15:4); and "If anyone loves Me,...We will come to him and make an abode with him" (14:23). How can we live in Him, and how can He live in us? The only way was for Him to become the Spirit. John 15 needs Romans 8 as its continuation. Without Romans 8, it is not sufficiently clear how to abide in the Lord. To abide in the Lord is to abide in the spirit, to set our mind on the spirit, and to walk closely according to the spirit. When we walk closely according to the spirit by setting our mind on the spirit, we abide in the spirit and also let the Lord abide in us. We should not wait until trials come and then begin to pray, asking the Lord for endurance and strength in order to be able to receive the breaking. At that point it is too late to ask for help, and praying will not be of any help. The fact that we turn to the Lord only when the trials come proves that we do not live in the spirit. If we were to live in the spirit, it would not matter whether we were experiencing trials, temptations, favor, pity, or anything else. They would all be the same to us, because we would simply be living in the spirit. No matter what kind of wind would blow on us—whether our wife would lose her temper or a brother would argue with us—we would not be shaken. We would just live by our Lord and live in the spirit.

NEEDING TO EXERCISE AND PRACTICE LIVING WITH THE LORD

This is an exceedingly simple way. The Lord became flesh and redeemed us from our sins. Then He resurrected and became the life-giving Spirit to be received by us. When we use our spirit to receive Him, He immediately comes into our spirit to regenerate us. Furthermore, in our spirit He also becomes our life, our life supply, and even our person. He and we have one life, one living, one move, and one action. We just live by Him. We do not know what it is to love the world and what it is to not love the world. We do not know what it is to hate others and what it is to love others. We do not know what it is to be proud and what it is to be humble. We just live by Him. This is what God intends to recover in this age. For many centuries this is what He has been after but has not been able to obtain. If you speak to people about redemption, victory, holiness, the cross, and breaking, they can understand. However, when you speak to them about living in the spirit, having one life and one living with the Lord twenty-four hours a day, it seems that they understand yet do not care. After understanding, no one exercises and practices it. After reading this chapter, how many of us will exercise in this matter? Tomorrow morning when a situation arises, we may forget this chapter and try again to endure, to love our wife, or to submit to our husband. There is no effect in us, and we do not have any response, because we do not have this matter in us.

In the Bible there is one book, the Gospel of John, which specifically shows us this matter. God became flesh to be the Lamb of God who accomplished redemption. Furthermore, after His death and resurrection, He became the breath of life and breathed Himself into us. When He gets into man, the Father also gets into man. When He gets into man, the Son also gets into man. He is in man as life, as bread, as living water, as spiritual air, and as a person. Man has one life and one living with Him, thereby living Him out. This is the story of God's relationship with man. This matter has been spoken a hundred times, even a thousand times, yet in our daily living, most of us do not practice it. We have heard many other teachings in the past, and we were willing to exercise and practice them. The only exception is the vision in the Gospel of John. It has been spoken, and we have heard it, but it has had no effect on us.

We in the church need a vision. We all need to see that it is not a matter of being holy or being victorious nor a matter of this or that. Today everything hinges on the fact that the

Triune God as the all-inclusive Spirit is in our spirit to be our life and our all. We live by Him, and He and we are one—one in life and one in living. He is us, and we are Him. The vine is not only Him but also us, because we are branches of the vine. If you could go and ask a branch, "What are you doing?" it would reply, "I do not know anything. I only know to live and remain in the vine, growing leaves when it is time to grow leaves, blossoming when it is time to blossom, and bearing fruit when it is time to bear fruit. Everything depends on the natural law of life. As a branch, I just need to abide in the vine. It is that simple."

We, however, have been so confused and mixed up because we have accumulated so many things within, such as human culture, religious concepts, ethical thoughts, and Christian doctrines. Some propose one thing while others suggest another thing. Some want to preach the gospel extensively, others desire to have more time to pray, and still others want to speak in tongues. We need to read the New Testament again. If we would read it in an unbiased way, we would bow our heads and say, "The fundamental thought, the central point, and the emphasis of the Bible is that God has become the life-giving Spirit, the all-inclusive Spirit." He has accomplished everything. He is waiting for us to receive Him into us. We all have a spirit to receive Him, and we all can live by Him. This is not a doctrine, an exhortation, or a religious regulation. Rather, this is a living Spirit, a living person, living in us, and we are living by Him. Everything is here. If we have this, we have everything.

LIVING IN THE SPIRIT BEING THE MOST SIMPLE, CONVENIENT, AND EXCELLENT WAY

Some of the saints have said to me, "Brother Lee, over twenty years ago when you were training us here in Taipei, you spoke something different." I answered these ones, "You are exactly right, but that was in 1953, and today it is 1975!" I admit that I have changed. In 1953 I learned a certain amount, but today I have learned more. The first time I went to America, I took the fastest airplane possible. It flew no more than three hundred miles per hour. It took twenty-six to twenty-seven hours to reach America, and I thought that that was very fast. Today, however, the jet planes can fly more than five hundred miles per hour, and it takes only around ten hours to fly from America to here. When I was on board a 747 jumbo jet, I felt as if I was at home. The ride was so comfortable, steady, and smooth. Would you prefer to take the 747, or would you still take the airplane built in 1946? If you would still prefer to take the out-of-date airplane, then you are very foolish. This does not mean that that kind of airplane is useless. It still has a little usefulness, but it is not as useful as the 747. In the past I spoke about pursuing holiness and pursuing victory. I gave nineteen messages on the experience of life, and every one of those messages is still valid to this day. Nevertheless, if I were to speak again, I would not need nineteen messages. I would only need to speak four words: "Living in the spirit." Living in the spirit is sufficient. If we live in the spirit, the lusts of the flesh will not be fulfilled. If we live in the spirit, we will drop the world spontaneously.

The most simple, convenient, and excellent way is to live in the spirit. The entire Gospel of John does not emphasize anything else. It just presents verses such as, "He...shall live because of Me," "Abide in Me," "Because I live, you also shall live," and, "In that day you will know that I am in My Father, and you in Me, and I in you" (6:57; 15:4; 14:19, 20). Then Romans 8 says, "Walk...according to the spirit" (v. 4). It is sufficient to live and walk according to the spirit. We need to exercise the spirit. The best way is to live in the spirit twenty-four hours a day. Then when we come to the meeting, we will be able to express something in spirit. Our spirit will have been exercised to the point that it is living and refreshing, and it will have a rich store to enable us to function in the meeting in any way that we desire. If we want to praise, there will be praise. If we want to pray, there will be prayer. If we want to minister the word, there will be the word. If we want to testify, there will be testimonies. We will not be like what we are today—not living in the spirit for most of the day and living in the spirit only when it is almost time to go to the meeting and when we must begin to prepare ourselves. This is why it is extremely difficult for us to speak anything in the meetings.

If we have seen the vision, we will see that the Lord's way today is to work Himself into us so that we may live by Him. It is not a matter of living by Him in the mind but of living by Him in the spirit. If we would live by Him in this way day by day, our spirit would be living, flowing, and efficient. Moreover, we would be rich in experience and able to express those riches accordingly. In this way the church meetings will be delivered from ordinances. This is what we need to see today. This way is the Lord's way, the proper way, for the preparation of His bride and for His coming back.

CHAPTER FOUR

THE BRINGING FORTH OF THE NEW MAN AND LIVING IN THE SPIRIT

Scripture Reading: Eph. 2:15; 3:8, 16-17a, 19b; 4:23-24; 2 Cor. 3:18

KEEPING UP-TO-DATE WITH THE FLOW OF THE AGE

During the Chinese War of Resistance against the Japanese, I traveled to the northwestern provinces of China to visit the churches. In some of the places I had to ride on a large handcart that could cover only about fifty kilometers after traveling the whole day from dawn to evening. At night, upon arriving at an inn, it seemed like all my bones had been detached. All I could do was lie down and go to sleep. Traveling in those days was truly a hardship. Today, however, both Taiwan and the United States have well-built highways and excellent transportation systems. Therefore, traveling in these countries is efficient and comfortable. This is a very practical illustration of how the age changes. I have been a Christian for fifty years already. In the first few years it seemed as if I was riding on a large handcart. I tried so hard to pursue, yet I did not advance much, I did not learn many lessons, nor did I have much growth in life. Then, gradually, the Lord led us through many changes, and today we can see that we have covered a great distance. Our messages and hymns are much more advanced than what we formerly had. We are truly in a different age. Regrettably, the churches in the Far East have not stayed up-to-date with the flow of the age. I am deeply concerned that the messages being released in many localities may be short of revelation, not rich enough, and not up-to-date.

Some of the saints refuse to follow the flow of the age. They declare that they want to receive everything firsthand instead of learning from others. This kind of talk is deceptive. Only a few people, like Paul, received everything firsthand. Thus, everything that is taken from the Scriptures is no longer firsthand. Honestly, I do not care whether or not I receive something firsthand. All I care about is the object itself. If the object is a diamond, I do not care how many hands it has passed through. As long as it is in my hand, it is valuable to me. However, if the object were dung, I would not want it, even if I was the first to receive it. We all need to be humble, not thinking that we have seen something. Although we surely have seen some things, what we have seen may be worthless. We need to see the central vision, which is the vision that the Triune God became flesh, died for the accomplishment of redemption, and in resurrection became the all-inclusive life-giving Spirit. Today He has entered into our spirit and lives in us. He not only gives His life to us but also puts Himself into us to be our person. He and we are joined together, having one life, one living, one walk, and one move, and we simply live by Him. This is the most important matter.

Some may say that they have learned a particular lesson, such as how to be holy. These kinds of lessons, however, are peripheral matters. It does not make much difference whether we learn them or not. Today God has a central purpose, a central vision, which we need to see. This is what the children of God lack today. This is lacking not only in Christianity but even among us. We all need to see this.

THE CHURCH BEING THE NEW MAN
CREATED WITH THE LIFE OF CHRIST

Ephesians is a book specifically on the church. Many people know that Ephesians 1 says that the church is the Body of Christ (v. 23). How many know, however, that the church is the new man? Ephesians 2:15 says that Christ, having solved all the problems on the cross, created the Jewish believers and the Gentile believers in Himself into one new man. This new man must be a corporate entity, because there is only one new man, not many new men. This new man was created by Christ in Himself. What material did Christ use to create the new man? He used Himself as the material. The Lord Jesus created all of us into one new man with Himself as the material. The Greek word for *create* implies to create something new. Previously there was no such thing as the new man in the universe. Now, however, Christ has created the new man in Himself with His resurrection life. Before His death and resurrection, our Lord had the eternal life of God, but He did not have the life that had passed through death and resurrection. The Lord Jesus created the new man not with the eternal life that had not passed through death but with the eternal life that had passed through death and resurrection. There is a great difference between the life that has passed through death and the life that has not passed through death. Before His crucifixion He already had the eternal life, but that life had not entered into death, passed through death, and come out of death again. After His resurrection He had the eternal life that had passed through death and entered into resurrection. It was with such an eternal life that the Lord Jesus created the one new man. Therefore, anyone who belongs to the new man has passed through death and is in resurrection.

NEEDING TO SEE AND ENJOY
THE UNSEARCHABLE RICHES OF CHRIST

After this, Ephesians 3 tells us that Paul was sent to announce to us the unsearchable riches of Christ (v. 8). The unsearchable riches of Christ are contained in His eternal life, a life that has passed through death and resurrection. All His riches are in this eternal life. We need someone to help us so that our eyes may be opened to see this. We need someone to unveil the contents of this life and to show us the vision of the riches of Christ, scene after scene. The elements of the new man within us are exceedingly rich! The unsearchable riches are right within us today!

How can we enjoy these riches? In the latter part of chapter 3 Paul prayed for us, asking the Father to grant us, according to the riches of His glory, to be strengthened with power through His Spirit into the inner man (v. 16). God has glory, and His glory is rich. The riches of His glory are the unsearchable riches of Christ. Notice that Ephesians 3 refers to riches twice. First it speaks of the unsearchable riches of Christ, and then it speaks of the riches of God's glory. The riches spoken of in these two places are one. Paul prayed that the Father would grant us, according to such riches, to be strengthened into the inner man with power through His Spirit, the all-inclusive Spirit. This means that within us there is something living, vital, and organic that continuously stirs us within, not in our mind but in our regenerated new man. As a result, Christ is able to make His home in our heart (v. 17a).

CHRIST MAKING HIS HOME IN OUR HEART

This matter of Christ making His home in our heart is not a small matter. It is not merely a parable or an illustration; it is a reality. Christ makes His home in our heart—not just in our spirit but in our heart, which surrounds our spirit. By reading the Scriptures we can see that our spirit is surrounded by our heart. First Peter 3 says that there is a hidden man of our heart (v. 4). That hidden man is our spirit. Our spirit is in the inner part of our heart, and our heart surrounds our spirit. If our spirit is strengthened, then Christ can make His home not only in our spirit but also in our heart. In other words, every part of our being may be occupied by Christ. This is not an ethical teaching, a religious teaching, or a philosophical teaching. This is a heavenly vision.

I am concerned that although many brothers and sisters have read Ephesians again and again, they may not have seen such a vision until now. They may not have seen that Christ is waiting in our spirit for an opportunity to saturate every part of our being with Himself so that He can make His home in our heart. Ephesians 3:19b says, "That you may be filled unto all the fullness of God." What kind of philosophy or doctrine is this? This is higher than any philosophy or doctrine! The Chinese Confucianists say that the principle of the highest level of learning is to develop the bright virtue. This principle at the most helps to develop our bright virtue, which is our innate knowledge and ability. Today we have not only the bright virtue, the innate knowledge and ability; we have the all-inclusive Christ, the all-inclusive Spirit, and the Triune God in our spirit as the unsearchable riches in us. Wang Yang-ming, a Chinese philosopher, said that if a person only makes outward improvements but neglects to develop his innate knowledge and ability, he is like a tree without roots and a stream without a source. If the philosophers pay so much attention to the matter of our inner source, how much more should we! What they pay attention to is only the innate knowledge and ability—the bright virtue within man. We, however, should focus on the great Triune God, the all-inclusive Christ, and the all-inclusive Spirit who dwells in our spirit and is mingled with us as one spirit.

If you truly see this vision, you will be beside yourself for at least three days because this is a tremendously great matter! The Triune God is right within us. The all-inclusive Spirit is right within us and has become one spirit with us. He has become me that I also may become Him. He and I, I and He, have one life, one living, one walk, and one move! Anyone who has seen this will jump up and down. Eventually, we will be filled unto all the fullness of God. We will not be filled with only a little love or with a little humility; we will be filled unto all the fullness of God. This is the living of the new man, and this is the church life.

CARING ONLY FOR THE RELEASE OF THE SPIRIT AND NOT HAVING REGULATIONS IN THE MEETINGS

If we would all live in this vision, there would be no regulations in our meetings. It is possible that in a given meeting no one would ever choose a hymn, but instead everyone would pray. In addition, we do not need to pray according to a set pattern. It is all right to pray only two or three sentences. Set patterns originate from the mind. Whatever we want to pray, we should simply pray. We are too accustomed to being in religion, not realizing that a set pattern is like a rope with which we hang ourselves. Why do we need a set pattern? It is because our spirit does not rise up. We kill the meeting, yet we do not know why the meeting has been killed. I do not mean that it is wrong to pray after singing a hymn. However, it is not proper if it becomes a set pattern.

The Lord in us is living. Every one of us has the living Lord within us. When we come to the meeting, why do we not allow the living Lord to take action? If we wait for a certain brother to call a hymn and wait for another brother to lead the prayer, we are meeting according to a set pattern and not according to the spirit. We often condemn the denominations, but today our practice has become the same as the practice in the denominations. Each brother and sister is like a pew member. When we come to a meeting, we should be releasing our spirit and worshipping God. If we would all live in the spirit, then when we come to a meeting, we would be quiet in the Lord's presence on the one hand and releasing our spirit on the other hand. Then there would be no fixed regulations. Instead, the riches would spontaneously flow out from every one of us. The aggregate of this flowing out would be our worship. This kind of meeting would be full of the expression of God, full of the presence of Christ, and full of the moving of the Holy Spirit. Moreover, all the saints would be fed. This is the church meeting. If our meetings were like this, then when people come into our midst, they would declare that God is among us (1 Cor. 14:25).

BEHOLDING THE LORD WITH UNVEILED FACE

We always tend to stick to our old rules, and these old rules always kill us. Second Corinthians 3:18 tells us that a normal condition is one of having an unveiled face. Yet so many people today are veiled. What is a veil? A veil is something that prevents you from seeing. Our old habits, old regulations, old concepts, and old experiences are all veils. We need to have an unveiled face. All the veils, from within our spirit to our outward being, must be taken away. In 2 Corinthians 3 the veil refers to the law, to knowledge, and to the teachings of the Old Testament. It is the same today. Our veils are our biblical knowledge, our biblical doctrines, and our old experiences. We all need to receive mercy in order that God may remove the veils from our face layer by layer so that we may have an unveiled face. Our face should be like an open mirror. If you were a mirror, when you beheld me, you would reflect my image. However, if as a mirror you were veiled, then you would lose your function. We often say that we need to lift up our heads and behold the Lord. However, if our face has layers and layers of veils upon it, we will be unable to see the Lord. We need an unveiled face. Our whole being, from our spirit to our outward being, needs to be unveiled to be like an open mirror, beholding and reflecting our Lord. Then His image will be imprinted on us as the mirror, and we will reflect His image and will be transformed into the same image from glory to glory, even as from the Lord Spirit.

It is good that the churches in Taiwan are all very steady. However, although our feet need to be steady, our spirit needs to be changeable. We need to change in our prayer, in our way of living, and in our coming together for fellowship. Everyone must change. Without change we will have no way! If we remain in our oldness, there will be no difference between the practices among us and the rituals in the denominations. We will know everything except the spirit, and we will have everything except the spirit. O Lord, remove our veils!

CHAPTER FIVE

GUARDING OURSELVES FROM IDOLS AND LIVING IN THE SPIRIT

Scripture Reading: 1 John 2:24, 27-28; 4:13; 5:4, 18-21; Heb. 4:12; 6:18-20

ABIDING IN THE LORD UNTIL HE COMES

The Triune God became the life-giving Spirit to abide in our spirit and to become one with us (1 Cor. 15:45; 6:17). Now He wants us to live by Him, having one life and one living with Him. I believe that we have all seen and heard this already. What we need is to look to the Lord that He may continue to grant us mercy and grace so that we would live according to what we have seen. It is not necessary to see this again or to seek some other method. We just need to live according to the vision we have seen.

First John 2:24 says, "As for you, that which you heard from the beginning, let it abide in you. If that which you heard from the beginning abides in you, you also will abide in the Son and in the Father." We should appreciate the words *abide* and *abides*. If we let that which we heard from the beginning abide in us, we will abide in the Son and in the Father. This speaking is not of the earth but of the heavens. One cannot hear this kind of speaking among human beings on earth. This kind of speaking is from the heavens. It is amazing that we can abide in the Son and in the Father. The apostle John says, "Little children, abide in Him" (v. 28). This does not mean to abide for just one day or three days but to abide until He comes.

To abide in the Lord is not just to stay in Him but to live and move in Him. Since we have heard this eternal mystery, from now on we should simply abide in the Lord, living and walking in Him. Do not ask how to abide in the Lord. Simply abide in the Lord. If you have been saved, then you have the Lord in you, and you will surely know how to abide in Him. Therefore, do not study. Simply abide in the Lord. We need to abide in Him until He comes.

A MYSTERIOUS FACT—THE LORD BEING IN US

In God's economy there is a great fact that we are often not conscious of and do not care much about. This fact is that when we repented and believed into the Lord, the Lord as the living Spirit entered into us in an imperceptible way. If you do not believe this, you can try an experiment. Try to say, "I do not feel that the Lord is abiding in me. I do not want Him, and I do not believe in Him anymore." If you would try such an experiment, immediately you would discover that the Lord is in you. The more you would say, "I do not believe anymore," the more the Lord would say, "You cannot do that. I have to remain here." You may say, "I do not want Jesus anymore," but He would say, "I want you." If you would try this, you would realize that there is such a person in you. The unbelievers do not have such a person in them. How can we tell who are believers in Christ and who are not? We cannot judge merely by outward appearance. The believers have a mysterious person in them. This is truly a very mysterious matter.

There are millions of people throughout the world today who have believed in Jesus, yet none of them have seen the Lord Jesus with their eyes. In a sense, we have seen Him in spirit. Outwardly, however, none of us have seen Him. Nevertheless, within us is something that makes it impossible for us to stay away from Him. Even if we were to fall and become degraded to the extent that we appeared improper to others, this mysterious person would still be in us. The more we say, "I do not believe in Him, I do not want Him, I do not care about Him, and I do not care for Him," the tighter He will hold us within. This proves that something mysterious has happened in us—the wonderful One, the all-inclusive Lord Spirit, has entered into us.

THE LORD DESIRING ONLY THAT WE LIVE BY HIM

The Lord's desire is not that we would be zealous and that we would do this or that for Him. Rather, His desire is that we would be one with Him and live by Him. He is our life and our person. Eventually, He wants to become us, and He also wants us to become Him. This is a very simple matter, yet we are not willing to do it.

To be saved is very simple. We are not required to do many things. All that is required of us in order to be saved is that we believe. Once we believe, we are saved. The unique sin of the unbelieving Gentiles before the Lord is their unbelief. Sinners will go to hell not because they stole and robbed but because they did not believe in the Lord. Sinners will perish mainly because of one sin—unbelief. We believers also have one sin—not living by the Lord. With the unbelievers, their main sin is their unbelief. With us believers, our main sin is our not living by the Lord. Simply speaking, we do not live in the spirit.

We may pray, read the Word, attend meetings, work for the Lord, serve Him, and worship Him, yet most of the time we do not remain in the spirit and live by the Lord Jesus. We need to drop our religious views. We should not think that it is good enough just to pray, read the Word, attend meetings, serve, and worship. We should never think this way. This is our religious view. It is very possible to be outside the spirit and apart from the Lord while praying, reading the Word, or meeting and worshipping. We may do all these things yet not be in the spirit. Then our worship becomes something religious, something done to God without God in it, and our service becomes religious, something that is a service to the Lord but lacks the Lord in it. We may have religion but may not have the Lord and may not be in the spirit.

THE TEMPLE AND THE MANGER

Before the Lord Jesus came to the earth, there was already a temple in the city of Jerusalem, built according to God's ordination. It was exclusively for the worship of God. In front of the temple there was an altar. The priests, having been trained to serve, served daily in the outer court, wearing their priestly garments and offering sacrifices according to the order of each one's course. Moreover, they also went into the Holy Place to burn the incense, light the lamps, and arrange the table of the bread of the Presence for the worship of God. Undoubtedly, there was a set pattern of orthodox worship. However, one day God came as the Lord Jesus. When He came, He did not go to the temple. Instead, He went to a manger in a little city called Bethlehem. At that moment, where was God? Was He in the temple, or was He in the manger? Was the worship that was being carried out in the temple true or false? It is difficult to say. On the surface the worshipping in the temple was true worship, but intrinsically, people could not touch God, because God was not there. Instead, He was in the manger. He grew up in Nazareth and then went forth to preach the word. One day He went to Bethany to visit a brother and two sisters in a little house. He went into that house and fellowshipped with them. At the same time, the priests in the temple were busy offering sacrifices and burning incense. Where was God at that time? He was not in the temple but in Bethany, in that little house. Where was the true worship being rendered? It was being rendered not in the temple but in Bethany. The worship in the temple was fundamental, scriptural, orderly, proper, imposing, and impressive. Everyone recognized it as the true worship. No one would have acknowledged that what was taking place in the little house in Bethany—three young people sitting casually before the Lord Jesus and talking with Him in a natural way—was a form of worship. People would have said that they were too loose, that they did not put on priestly garments or offer sacrifices, or that they were too casual. We all should see this picture clearly. The true worship depends not on outward ceremonies but on the inward reality. If the Lord is in something, it is worship. If He is not, it is a religious ceremony.

EVERYTHING BEGOTTEN OF GOD
KEEPING ITSELF FROM SINNING

The first Epistle of John may seem like a shallow book, a book that is not very deep. Actually, the first Epistle of John is one of the most mysterious books in the Bible. It says that we can abide in the Lord, which is truly something mysterious. It also says that there is something within us that "has been begotten of God" (5:4a). The Gospel of John shows us what this is. John 3:6 says, "That which is born of the flesh is flesh, and that which is born of the Spirit is spirit." What is this thing that has been begotten of God? It is the regenerated spirit within us. The spirit in us is that which has been born of God. There is only one thing in the whole universe that has been begotten of God. It is in you, it is in me, and it is in every believer in the Lord. The word for *everything* used in 1 John 5:4 was chosen very carefully. It is important to properly translate this Greek word as *everything*. Without this verse we simply cannot understand the first Epistle of John. I read 1 John 3:9 for decades without knowing why it says that everyone who has been begotten of God does not sin. I did not understand this, because although we have been begotten of God, according to our experience, we still commit sins.

In modern Christianity there is a school of thought that teaches the eradication of sin. Those who teach this say that once a person believes in the Lord, sin is eradicated from him. They base this teaching on 1 John 3:9, which says, "Everyone who has been begotten of God does not practice sin,...and he cannot sin." Therefore, they say that once you are born of God, sin is eradicated from you, so you cannot sin anymore. Forty years ago in Shanghai there was an elderly man who adhered to this school of thought. He spoke about regeneration in a very strong way, telling people that they had to be born again. However, he also told people that once they were regenerated, sin was eradicated from them, and they could no longer sin. One day he took four young people to a park. Tickets were required to enter the park, yet that elderly man bought only two tickets. Two of the young men entered the park using the two tickets. Then one of the two came out with the tickets and then entered the park again with another young man. This was repeated until all five people had entered the park using the same two tickets. One of the young men related this incident to me. When he saw this situation, he was perplexed, wondering how it could be right to buy only two tickets and bring five people into the park. He asked himself, "What is this?" After they returned, he asked the elderly man, "Has not sin been eradicated from us? Then how could we use only two tickets to bring five people into the park?" The elderly man replied, "This is not a sin. It is merely a weakness."

Whether it is a sin or a weakness, neither is good. After a person has been saved through regeneration, experientially speaking, he still can sin. Even 1 John says that to this day we still have the lust of the flesh, the lust of the eyes, and the vainglory of life (2:16). Why is it then that chapter 3 says, "Everyone who has been begotten of God does not practice sin" (v. 9)? For many years we were unclear about this matter.

One day as I was reading 1 John and studying the Greek text, I came to verse 4 of chapter 5, which says, "Everything that has been begotten of God overcomes the world." It was then that the light came, and suddenly I was able to understand what was once unclear to me. The word *everything* refers to every person who has been begotten of God. Such an expression, however, refers especially to the part within a person that has been regenerated with the divine life, that is, the spirit of a regenerated person. The regenerated spirit of a believer does not practice sin (3:9), and it overcomes the world. The only thing in the universe that has been begotten of God is our spirit. Our flesh and our soul, including our mind, emotion, and will, were not begotten of God. "That which is born of the flesh is flesh, and that which is born of the Spirit is spirit" (John 3:6). No one can deny that the spirit in us has been begotten of God. Eventually, after checking with our experience, we must say Amen to this word. Our flesh can sin, as well as our mind, but our regenerated spirit cannot practice sin. In fact, while our flesh is sinning, our regenerated spirit continually warns us, "Do not sin! Do not sin!" The spirit always admonishes us. When we go along with our lust and go to see a movie, the spirit within us may say, "Go home! Do not watch anymore!" After we were saved, we found that there was something that always bothered us and gave us no peace. That was the regenerated spirit in us. Our regenerated spirit constantly bothers us. There is only one piece of land in this universe that is still clean, that has been reserved by God, and that does not have Satan's footprints on it. This piece of land is our regenerated spirit.

Regardless of how much the sisters love the world and its fashion, and regardless of how much they love to make themselves look pretty, their spirit will often speak from within, "Forget about all these things! Do not do all these meaningless things! Why do you spend so much time on these things?" We all have had this kind of experience. A strong sister may suffer a great temptation, and as a result, simply ignore the feeling in her spirit. She might say, "I do not care. Anyway, one day I will go to heaven. I do not believe that I will go to hell just for trying to make myself pretty. I am a young lady. I should not make myself look like an old woman." However, her spirit will still say to her, "It is useless to argue. Do not do this anymore! You will make the Lord unhappy." She will sense there is something within her that will not let her go.

In a way, I do not care whether we have overcome or failed. I hope we would all realize that there is something in us that has been begotten of God—our spirit. We may be in the worst place in the world, but our spirit will still say, "Get out of here! Stop fooling around here! How meaningless this is!" We may say that this is the Lord Jesus speaking to us. However, where is He when He speaks to us? He speaks to us not in our mind or in our emotions but in our regenerated spirit. Everything that has been begotten of God overcomes the world.

Furthermore, 1 John 5:18 says, "He who has been begotten of God keeps himself." As regenerated believers, we have been begotten of God specifically in our spirit. Thus, our regenerated spirit, as that which has been begotten of God, keeps us from sinning. We all can testify that many times we have been kept by this spirit which has been begotten of God. Many Christians have had such experiences. Perhaps while you were on your way to a movie theater, something within you said, "Go home! What are you coming here for?" After you entered the theater, something within said again, "Go home!" Eventually, you had to say, "Forget about this!" Thus, you went home. Who kept you? Who brought you back home? It was the regenerated spirit within you that kept you. We are all vile sinners and are all capable of committing gross sins, yet all these

years we have been kept. This is because our regenerated
spirit has kept us. Within us we have something that has been
regenerated, something that has been begotten of God. This
something is our spirit.

What is within this spirit? God Himself is in it. First John
3:9 says that it is God's seed, that is, God Himself and Christ
Himself. This is a very mysterious matter. In our regenerated
spirit is God Himself and Christ Himself as our seed. All we
need to do is to abide in our regenerated spirit and to live and
walk in our spirit. First John tells us that we have something
that has been regenerated. We have God's seed in our regenerated spirit. Thus, we need to abide in our regenerated spirit.
If we do, then we are of God.

THE WHOLE WORLD EXCEPT OUR SPIRIT
LYING IN THE EVIL ONE

First John also tells us that the whole world lies in the evil
one (5:19). The world includes the events, things, and people of
the world. In God's eyes the whole world—all human beings,
all human societies, and all things—is under the hand of Satan.
The only exception is our regenerated spirit. We should not
think that the unbelievers are under the authority of Satan
and that we are not. We cannot speak in such a general way.
It is possible that our mind is still under Satan's authority
and that only our regenerated spirit is not. Actually, it is very
possible that even our reading of the Word and our prayer are
under Satan's authority, because they may come not out of our
regenerated spirit but out of our mind, emotion, and prefer-
ence. I hope that we would be under a finer, deeper light. Only
one thing in the whole universe and on the whole earth does
not have Satan's footprints on it—our regenerated spirit. Aside
from our regenerated spirit, all the other parts of our being
are under the hand of Satan.

Let us consider again the illustrations given earlier. For
example, let us consider the day the Lord Jesus went to the
little house in Bethany and sat down to fellowship with His
disciples. At that very moment, the high priest in Jerusalem
was offering sacrifices and burning incense. Where was God
at that time? He was in the house in Bethany, not in the temple

in Jerusalem. Then how should we consider the worship in the
temple? Was it merely something religious? Actually, the high
priest's service, the burning of the incense, and the worship in
the temple were under the hand of the evil one. Therefore,
although the Jews were worshipping God and learning the
Scriptures in their synagogues, in Revelation 2 and 3 the Lord
Jesus called the Jews "a synagogue of Satan" (2:9; 3:9). The
Jewish synagogues had become synagogues of Satan. The synagogue not only became something religious but even became
the synagogue of Satan, because although that was where the
Jews worshipped God, studied the Scriptures, and served God,
God was not there. God was in another place—Bethany. Where
is today's Bethany? Today's Bethany is right within our spirit.
If we would consider this matter from such a perspective and
angle, we would immediately realize that any worship or service that is without the Lord Spirit is of the devil. This is a
solemn matter!

We must ask ourselves whether the Lord is in our prayer,
our reading of the Bible, and our bread-breaking meeting. If we
are not in the spirit and no one else is in the spirit, then the
Lord is not in these things, and all these things are still under
Satan's hand. Not only our dancing, going to nightclubs, and
playing mah-jongg are under Satan's hand, but even our reading of the Word, our prayer, and our going to meetings can be
under Satan's hand unless they are done in the spirit. This
is because the only thing in the whole universe that does not
have Satan in it is our regenerated spirit. Unless we are in our
spirit, whatever we do is under Satan's hand.

Where is God today? He is right in our spirit. We must see
that our spirit is God's Holy of Holies. The three parts of our
being—our spirit, our soul, and our body—correspond exactly
to the three parts of the tabernacle. Our spirit is the Holy of
Holies, and God's habitation in the heavens is also the Holy
of Holies. According to Hebrews, these two realms are connected. God's habitation, the place where God dwells, is the
Holy of Holies. Today our spirit is also the Holy of Holies. Our
spirit as the Holy of Holies is connected and joined to the
Holy of Holies in the heavens. If this were not so, we would
not be able to enter the Holy of Holies and touch the throne of

grace for timely help, as mentioned in Hebrews 4:16. If God's Holy of Holies were only in the heavens and not in our spirit, we would have no way to behold the Lord every day. However, our spirit today is the Holy of Holies.

Furthermore, the totality of all our spirits is the church. The church is not in a physical building. The church is in our spirit. The church is God's Holy of Holies because the church is the aggregate of the regenerated spirits of all the saints.

Therefore, when we pray, read the Word, worship, and serve, we must be in our spirit and in the church, because the church is the aggregate of our spirits. Sometimes we are not in the spirit, yet we come together to worship. At such a time, we must realize that our worship is not the worship in the church. If we are in such a situation, we are no longer inside the Holy of Holies but outside. Only our regenerated spirit as the Holy of Holies is not under the authority of Satan. Besides our regenerated spirit, everything else in the universe and on this globe has been defiled by Satan.

THIS BEING THE TRUE GOD AND ETERNAL LIFE

If we would read the last section of 1 John 5 again, we would understand its real significance. Verse 18 says, "We know that everyone who is begotten of God does not sin, but he who has been begotten of God keeps himself, and the evil one does not touch him." *Everyone who is begotten of God* refers not to the entire being of a regenerated believer but to his regenerated spirit. In this entire universe God has drawn a line around one thing—our spirit. I am convinced that God has done such a thing. God has set a limit for Satan, saying, "Satan, this is off limits to you! Do not transgress this boundary!"

We can see this principle in the book of Job. God permitted Satan to do this and that, yet He also set a boundary and forbade Satan from going beyond it. If we would carefully read the New Testament and also check with our experience, we would see that God has indeed drawn a boundary. The evil one cannot touch man's regenerated spirit. First John states very clearly that "he who has been begotten of God keeps himself, and the evil one does not touch him." As long as we remain in our regenerated spirit, we will be kept, and Satan will have no way in us. This does not mean that Satan will not try to use any of his schemes. On the contrary, he will try every possible way, but in the end he will have no way. Therefore, once we get into our spirit, we can say, "Satan, think of another way! Do you have any other ways?" Then Satan would say, "I have lost. I have exhausted all my ways. I would have a way if you were in your soul. I would have a way if you were in your mind. I would have many ways if you were in your flesh. But once you turn to your spirit, I have no way. I cannot harm you. I cannot touch you."

Verse 19 says, "We know that we are of God, and the whole world lies in the evil one." The whole world is like a fish lying on a chopping block, about to be cut up by the chef as he wishes. Only our regenerated spirit is not under Satan's hand. Besides this, everything else, including our flesh, our mind, our emotion, and our will, are all under Satan's hand.

Verse 20 says, "We know that the Son of God has come and has given us an understanding that we might know Him who is true." *Him who is true* refers to the Triune God, the all-inclusive Christ, and the all-inclusive Spirit. To know this One is to have real understanding. Although the professors and the people with doctorate degrees have the knowledge in the world, many will not come to receive the Lord Jesus. Thus, they do not have the real understanding. We, however, have the real understanding. Verse 20 continues, "We are in Him who is true, in His Son Jesus Christ. This is the true God and eternal life." Notice that this verse does not say, "He is." It says, "This is." The word *this* refers to this particular matter, circumstance, or situation, which is the true God and eternal life. There is only one thing in the whole universe that is real— the real God and eternal life.

GUARDING OURSELVES FROM IDOLS

Finally, there is a warning: "Little children, guard yourselves from idols" (v. 21). This means that anything that is not of the true God, not of the eternal life, and not in the regenerated spirit is an idol. Our reading of the Bible may be an idol, our prayer may be an idol, and even our bread-breaking may be an idol, because we may be reading the Word, praying, worshipping, serving, and even breaking bread outside of our regenerated spirit! We may be lying in the evil one because we are not in the spirit.

In His seventh epistle in Revelation 3 the Lord seemed to be saying to the church in Laodicea, "O Laodicea! I am ready to spew you out of My mouth. You are neither cold nor hot, so I will spew you out. Do you know that I am standing at the door and knocking? I am not inside of you but outside of you, and you are not in Me." Under such circumstances, the church in Laodicea was lying in the evil one. Practically speaking, the Laodiceans were not in the Lord, and the Lord was not in them. I am concerned that many times the churches are not in the Lord even while they are breaking the bread and that the Lord is not in the churches in the breaking of bread. The result is Laodicea. They have the teachings, the knowledge, and the rituals of worship, but they are not in the spirit, and the Lord is not in them. This is a serious matter!

First John 5:21 says, "Little children, guard yourselves from idols." You may say that there are no idols in your meeting hall. However, you may not realize that your idols are yourselves, your scheming, and your domineering. You may not realize that your desire to win others over so that they will agree with you is an idol. You may not realize that your idol is your insistence on teaching others the spiritual experience you had three years ago. You may love your Bible and insist that others read it the same way you do. This is also an idol. Whatever is not in the spirit is an idol. Whatever is not of the spirit is an idol. If the elders and co-workers in a local church have opinions, they have idols. If we are in the spirit, we will not have any opinions. The Lord Jesus is one, and He is also one in our spirit, so there cannot be any opinion if we are in our spirit. Any church in which there is dissension between the elders and the deacons, among the elders themselves, or between the elders and the co-workers, has idols.

What are idols? Whatever is not the true God is an idol. Today the true God is in our regenerated spirit. We abide in Him, and He also abides in us. This is the true God and the eternal life. When some responsible brothers are not in one

accord and are at a stalemate, that is an idol. When a few
brothers who serve together protect themselves from each
other, that is an idol. It is terrible to advertise the name of the
Lord Jesus yet sell our flesh.

For many years I did not understand why this word suddenly appeared at the end of 1 John: "Little children, guard
yourselves from idols." One day, however, the Lord showed me
this mystery, and then I realized that anything we do that
is not in the regenerated spirit and that does not live out the
Lord Spirit is an idol. Today there is only one true God, and
this true God is in only one place, that is, our spirit. Everything
outside of this spirit is an idol. If our bread-breaking and our
praising are not in the spirit, they are false. Our bearing of
responsibilities and our work may also be false if they are not
in the spirit. Our insistence with one another in our service is
also an idol.

FLEEING AND RIVER CROSSING

Hebrews 4 says that the word of God is living and able to
pierce through us, dividing our spirit, as the Holy of Holies,
from the soul that surrounds it (v. 12). Hebrews 6 says that
we are all fleeing (v. 18). From what are we fleeing? We are
fleeing from our idols, our flesh, our ideas, our views, our dissenting thoughts, and our old experiences. In the Greek text
the word for *fled* is used only twice in the New Testament. It
is used once in Acts 14:6, where the apostle Paul fled from
Iconium to Lystra and Derbe, and it is also used in Hebrews
6:18. The Greek word translated "fled" implies "to flee inten-
sively, seriously, and speedily," just as Lot and his wife fled
from Sodom. This is what the writer of the book of Hebrews
meant. He seemed to be saying, "O Hebrew brothers, you need
to flee! Flee from Judaism and your old doctrines."

Then where should we flee to? We should flee to the Holy
of Holies. We should flee from our disposition, our views
among the co-workers, and our dissenting thoughts. If we do
not flee, we will be under the hand of the devil. Our Fore-
runner has already entered into the spirit, into the Holy of
Holies. Today we should not remain in the outer court or in
the Holy Place. We all need to flee to the Holy of Holies, to the

presence of God. We must flee until we have nothing else to flee from, until we are directly touching God and are face to face with God. In this way we will be with God in the Holy of Holies. There will be no need for us to flee anymore. However, today we all must flee.

The word *Hebrew* means "river crosser." Abraham crossed a river. Hence, he was a river crosser. We all need to cross a river, to cross over from one side of the river to the other side. We need to cross the river of the flesh, the river of knowledge, the river of old religion, and the river of the old ways. May the Lord be merciful to us that we may be river crossers. We need to cross over to the land of Canaan, to enter into the rest where God's temple, God's sanctuary, is. The churches in the recovery have had a long history. Today they have come to the edge of the river. We must say, "O Lord, have mercy on us that we would flee into the Holy of Holies."

ABOUT THE AUTHOR

Witness Lee was born in 1905 in northern China and raised in a Christian family. At age 19 he was fully captured for Christ and immediately consecrated himself to preach the gospel for the rest of his life. Early in his service, he met Watchman Nee, a renowned preacher, teacher, and writer. Witness Lee labored together with Watchman Nee under his direction. In 1934 Watchman Nee entrusted Witness Lee with the responsibility for his publication operation, called the Shanghai Gospel Bookroom.

Prior to the Communist takeover in 1949, Witness Lee was sent by Watchman Nee and his other co-workers to Taiwan to ensure that the things delivered to them by the Lord would not be lost. Watchman Nee instructed Witness Lee to continue the former's publishing operation abroad as the Taiwan Gospel Bookroom, which has been publicly recognized as the publisher of Watchman Nee's works outside China. Witness Lee's work in Taiwan manifested the Lord's abundant blessing. From a mere 350 believers, newly fled from the mainland, the churches in Taiwan grew to 20,000 in five years.

In 1962 Witness Lee felt led of the Lord to come to the United States, and he began to minister in Los Angeles. During his 35 years of service in the U.S., he ministered in weekly meetings and weekend conferences, delivering several thousand spoken messages. Much of his speaking has since been published as over 400 titles. Many of these have been translated into over fourteen languages. He gave his last public conference in February 1997 at the age of 91.

He leaves behind a prolific presentation of the truth in the Bible. His major work, *Life-study of the Bible,* comprises over 25,000 pages of commentary on every book of the Bible from the perspective of the believers' enjoyment and experience of God's divine life in Christ through the Holy Spirit. Witness Lee was the chief editor of a new translation of the New Testament into Chinese called the Recovery Version and directed the translation of the same into English. The Recovery Version also appears in a number of other languages. He provided an extensive body of footnotes, outlines, and spiritual cross references. A radio broadcast of his messages can be heard on Christian radio stations in the United States. In 1965 Witness Lee founded Living Stream Ministry, a non-profit corporation, located in Anaheim, California, which officially presents his and Watchman Nee's ministry.

Witness Lee's ministry emphasizes the experience of Christ as life and the practical oneness of the believers as the Body of Christ. Stressing the importance of attending to both these matters, he led the churches under his care to grow in Christian life and function. He was unbending in his conviction that God's goal is not narrow sectarianism but the Body of Christ. In time, believers began to meet simply as the church in their localities in response to this conviction. In recent years a number of new churches have been raised up in Russia and in many European countries.